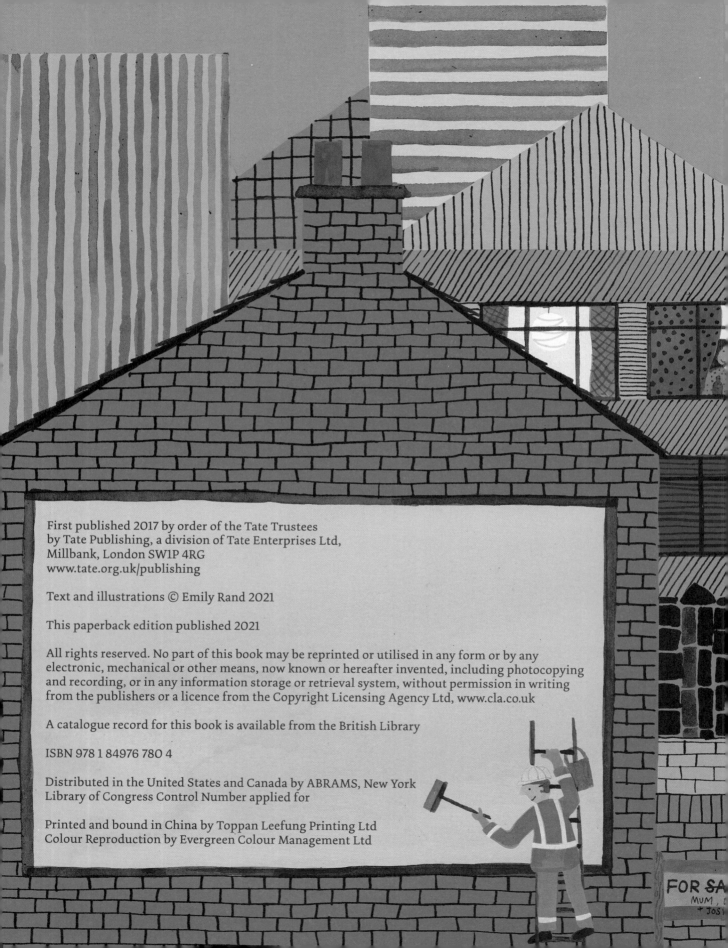

FOR SA
MUM,
+ JOS

In the Darkness of the Night

Emily Rand

Click goes the switch
As it turns off the light.
A hushed, gentle voice
Whispers "sleep tight".

As you lie in your bed
Curled up warm and tight,
Listen to the sounds
In the darkness of the night.

Down in the kitchen,
There's a clatter and a clink.
Dirty plates and dishes
Are being washed in the sink.

The house is now tidy,
The toys put away.
It's the end of another
Very long day.

A car door slams shut,
Someone's home late.
The jangle of keys
And the squeak of the gate.

The road is still, until...

Vrooooom!

A bike whizzes past
With a late night dinner.
It's going very fast!

Down in the street,
People laugh and shout
As they make their way home
From a fun night out.

Neon signs and street lamps
Fizz and burn so bright,
Lighting up the way
In the darkness of the night.

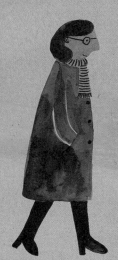

The late train rumbles by,
The day is now done,
But as some workers head home
For others it's just begun.

In an empty office block,
Somewhere near the top,
A lonely cleaner's humming
To the swishing of her mop.

In the distance a siren wails,
A police car speeds by
And a tired mother tries
To soothe her baby's cry.

Deep down underground,
Where no one can hear,
Fixing the tracks
Is the railway engineer.

The nurse works through the night,
So softly she treads,
As she checks on her patients
In their hospital beds.

In the early hours
Of the morning,
All is quiet indoors
Apart from the sound
Of low rumbling snores.

Outside loud squeals
And barks of city foxes,
As they search for food
In bins and in boxes.

As the moon slides by
To make way for the sun,
The sounds of the morning
Have only just begun.

The birdsong is silenced,
By the thunder of a plane
Bringing home its passengers
Back down to land again.

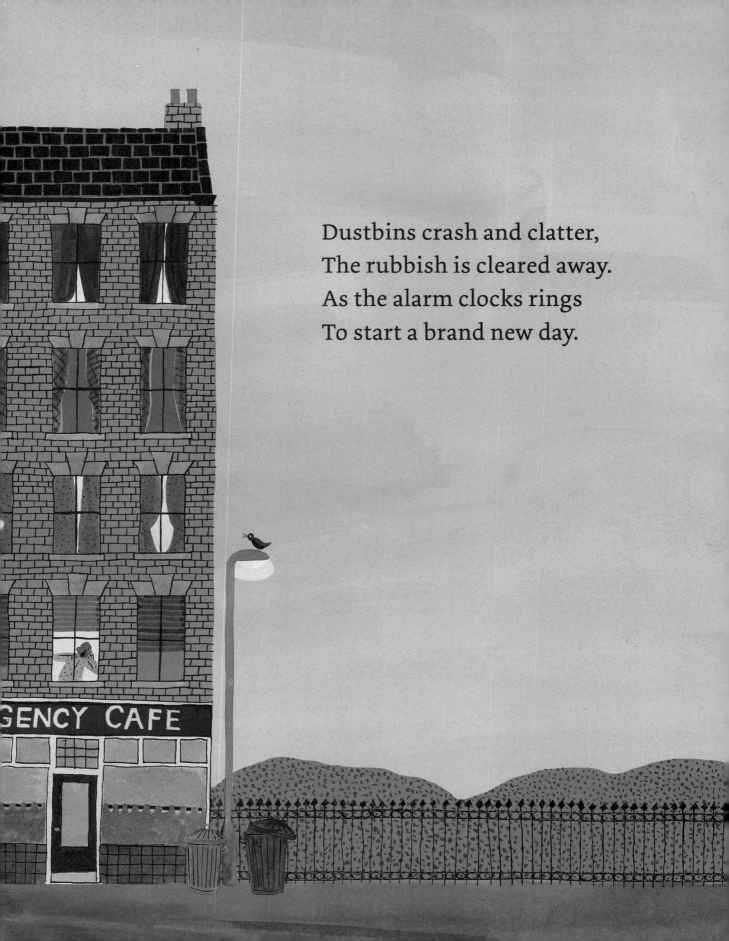

Dustbins crash and clatter,
The rubbish is cleared away.
As the alarm clocks rings
To start a brand new day.

The cheery postman
Whistles on his round.
Delivering the letters,
He makes a happy sound.

Pipes hum with water,
A splash from the tap.
A gurgle in the plughole,
The cat through the flap.

The trickle of the shower,
Footsteps on the floor
Time to get dressed.
It's daytime once more!

The curtains swish open!
It's time to say
"Hello" and "Good Morning"
To the brightness of the day.